Central Asian Sayings and Proverbs

Central Asia is a region stretching from the Caspian Sea to China, and from Iran to Russia in the north. The region consists of the former Soviet republics of Kazakhstan, Kyrgyzstan, Tajikistan, Turkmenistan, and Uzbekistan.

Central Asia has been a historic crossroads for the movement of people, goods, and ideas between Europe, West Asia, South Asia, and East Asia. Central Asia is an extremely large region of varied geography, including incredible high passes and mountains, vast deserts, and wonderous grassy steppes. The proverbs within this book come from this historical, rich region.

Kazakh Proverbs

Who a child will become is evident from an early age.

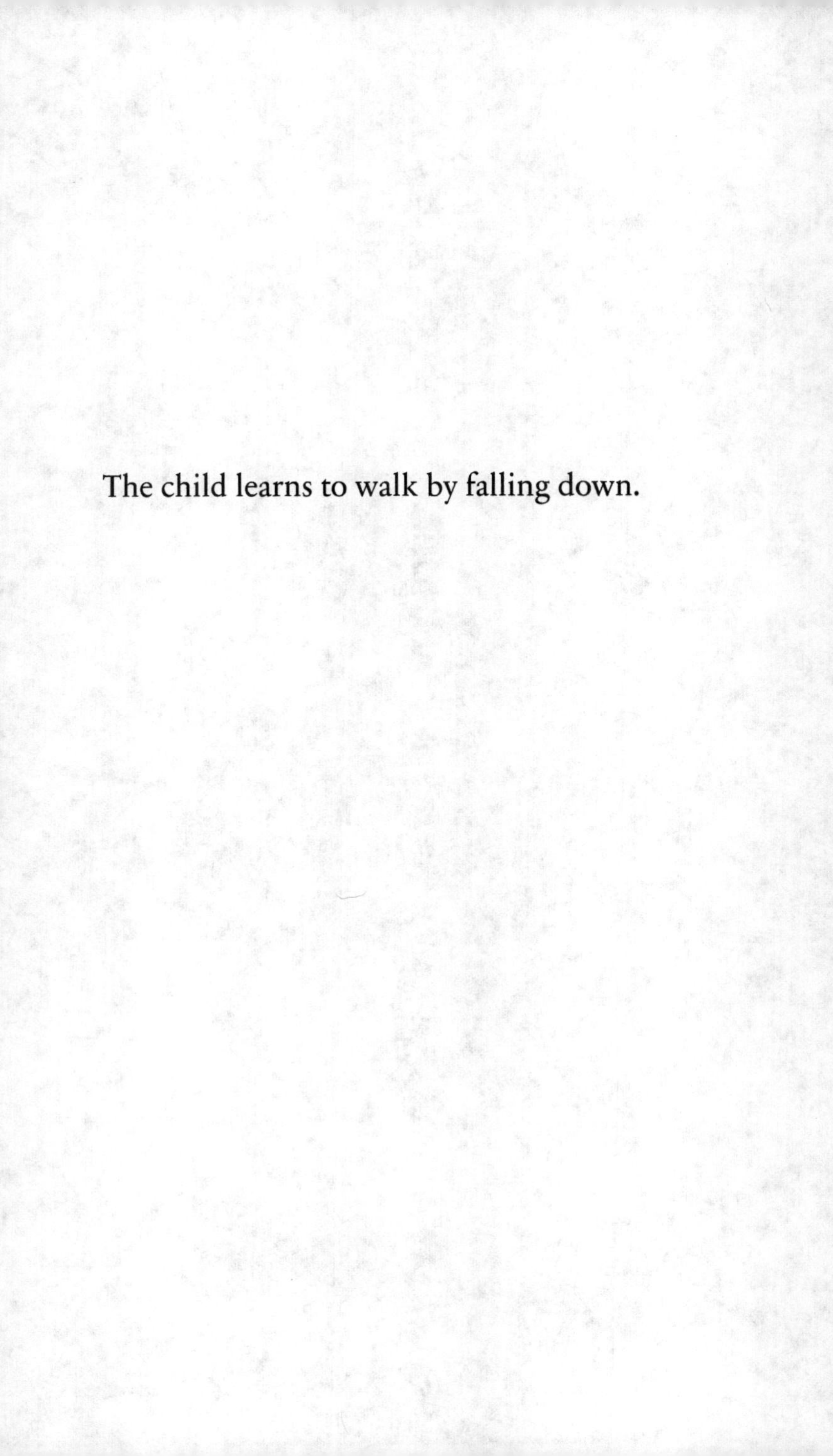

The child learns to walk by falling down.

To the crow his child appears white; to the hedgehog his child appears soft.

No matter how much you train the wolf, he still looks at the mountains and howls.

Even a mole feels strong when he is in his
hole.

As small as sparrow is, it still protects its
nest.

Who leads the people will swallow butter,
who lags behind the people will swallows
dust.

Kyrgyz Proverbs

If your right hand is angry, hold it back with your left.

A good wife is half of your life's happiness.

A wise man isn't one who has lived the longest, but has travelled the most.

A man grows old, but his courage does not.

A dog trusts its master; a bird trusts itself.

Knowledge builds up. Ignorance destroys.

Work is not a wolf.

Without difficulties, there is no reason to live.

Tajik Proverbs

For a greedy man even his grave is too small.

A woman's work is worth more than the talk
of a thousand men.

Do not confide in your friend if they have other friends.

Trying to hide lie will only make the affliction show on your face.

If you sit with the moon, you become the
moon.

Turkmen Proverbs

After the cart is broken, many people will offer advice on how to fix it.

The snake hates mint, but it still grows at
the entrance of its home.

Whatever you put in your pot comes to your spoon.

First God looks at the mountain, then He sends the snow.

If you don't step on a snake, it won't bite
you.

The person who spends time with the lame
learns how to limp.

Do not associate with a man whose pen
drips blood.

When you're sitting in a ship,
Don't quarrel with the ship's owner.

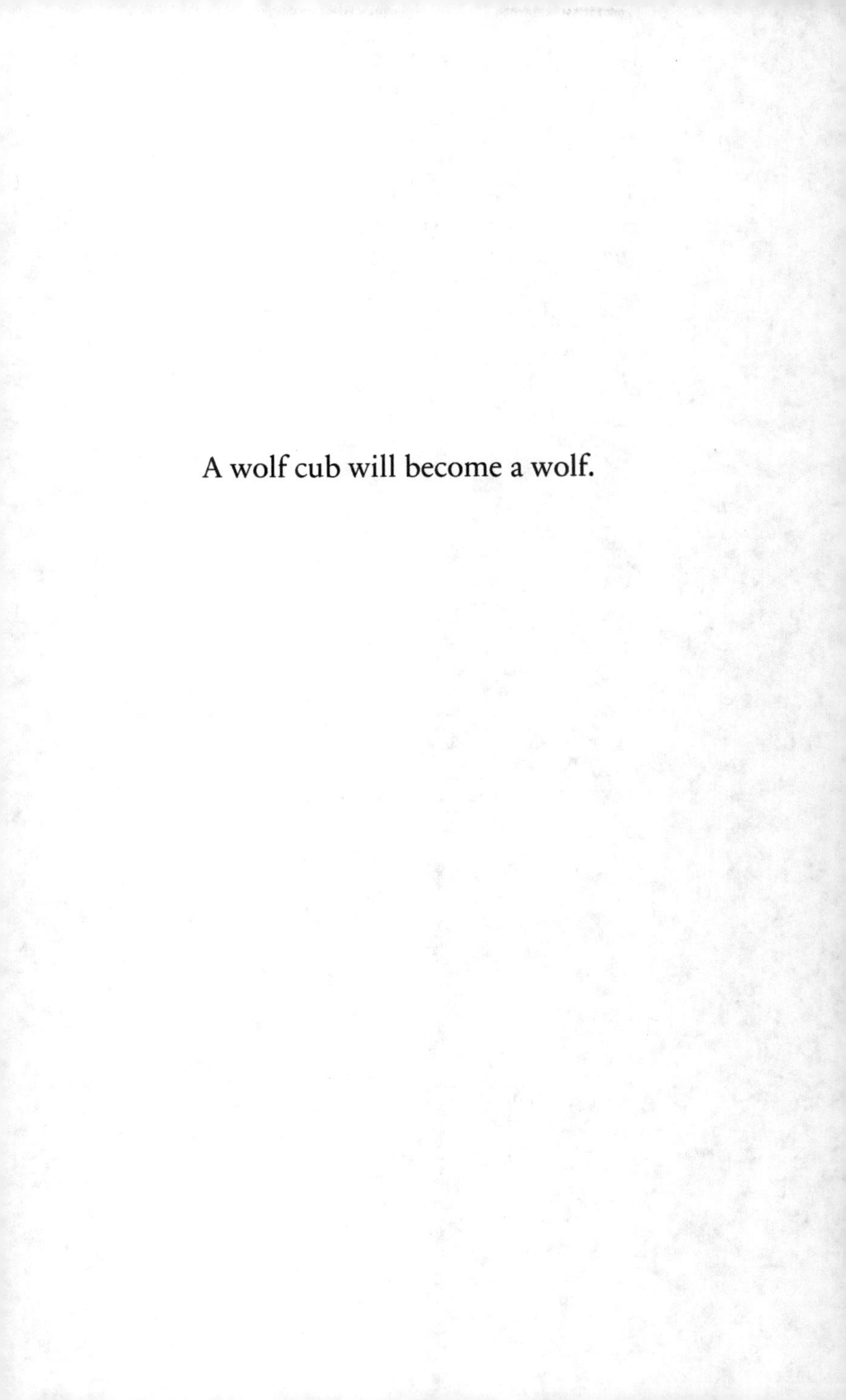

A wolf cub will become a wolf.

Grass grows from its own roots.

He eats with wolves and bleats with the
sheep.

If you are a master and I am a master, who
will milk the cows?

The goat may struggle against death, but the butcher thinks only of the fat.

When you are hungry, you don't think of
honor.

Just saying the word 'honey' will not make
your mouth sweet.

Uzbek Proverbs

Crows do not pick crows' eyes.

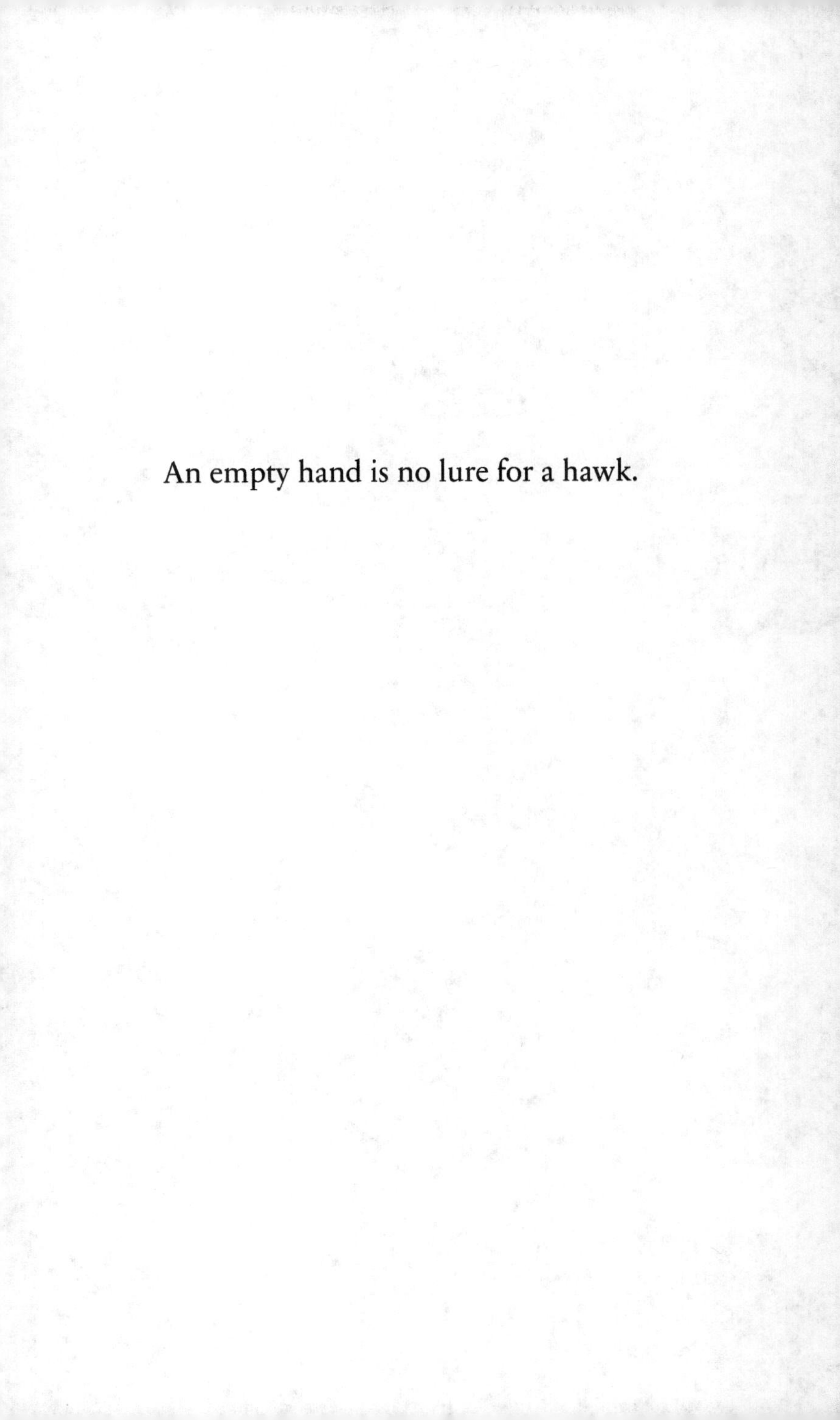

An empty hand is no lure for a hawk.

2023

Give your food to the people and they will pat your head. Give your food to the dogs, and they will gnaw your head.

Fatness is the right fit for a ram

Without reason no cat ventures out.

Don't choose a house, choose your neighbors. Don't choose a path, choose your traveling companions.

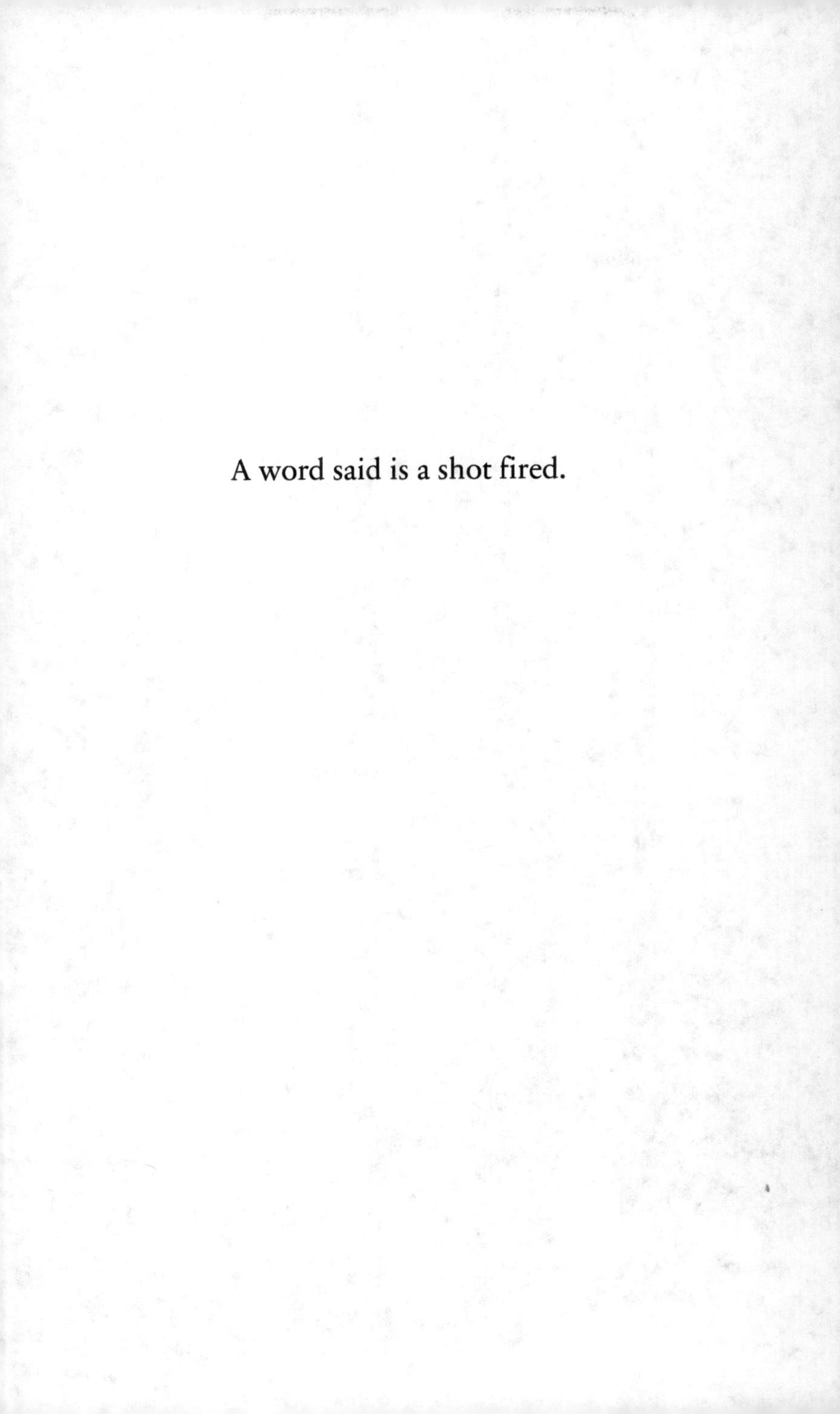

A word said is a shot fired.

He who speaks little knows much, for when they speak, it is with great thought.

Don't take gold, take knowledge, for knowledge is gold.

For a good man, it is not enough to be capable in forty professions.

Morning is wiser than evening.

Let the wet wood not be burned with the
dry.

www.ingramcontent.com/pod-product-compliance
Lightning Source LLC
Chambersburg PA
CBHW071643170726
48000CB00023B/824